A Cache of Jewels

and Other Collective Nouns

Written and illustrated by
RUTH HELLER

GROSSET & DUNLAP, NEW YORK

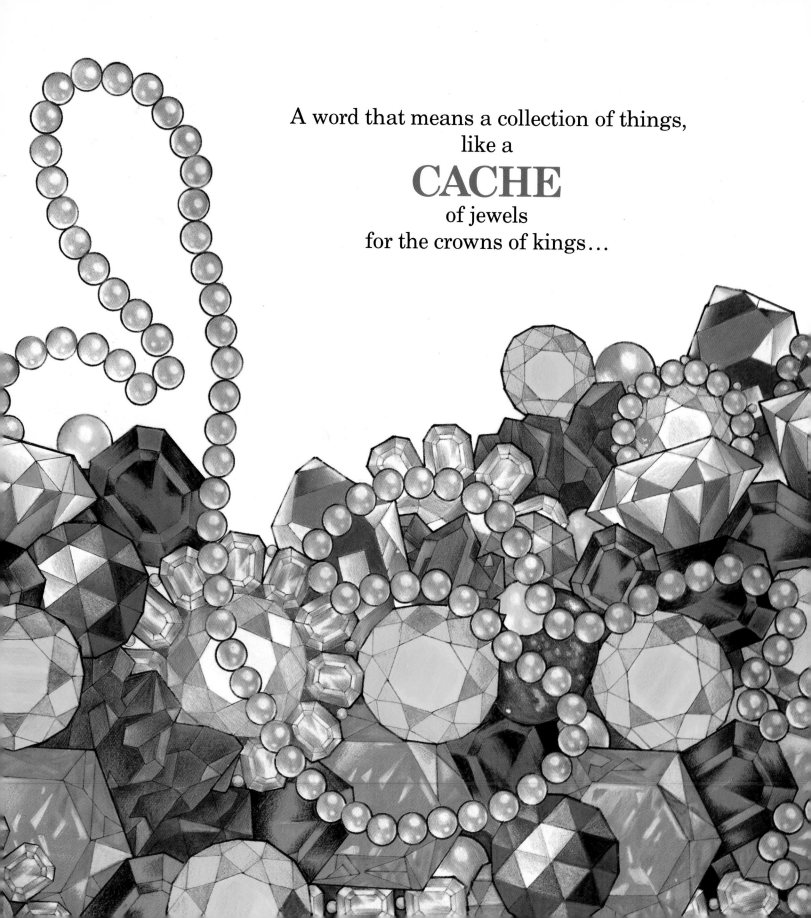

A word that means a collection of things,
like a
CACHE
of jewels
for the crowns of kings…

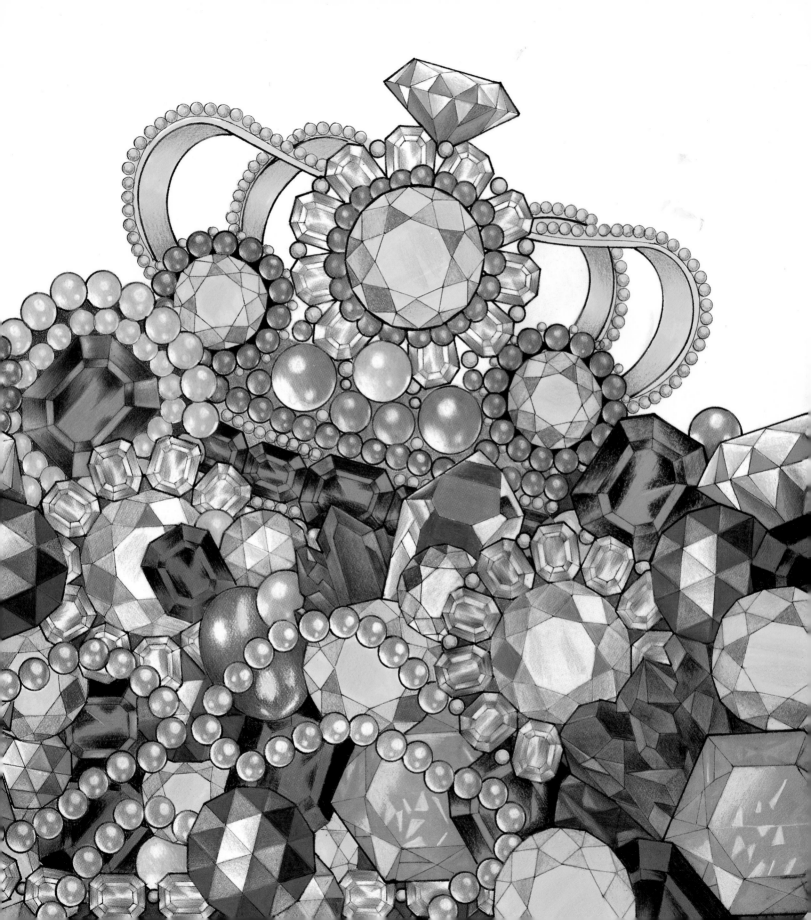

or a **BATCH** of bread all warm and brown,

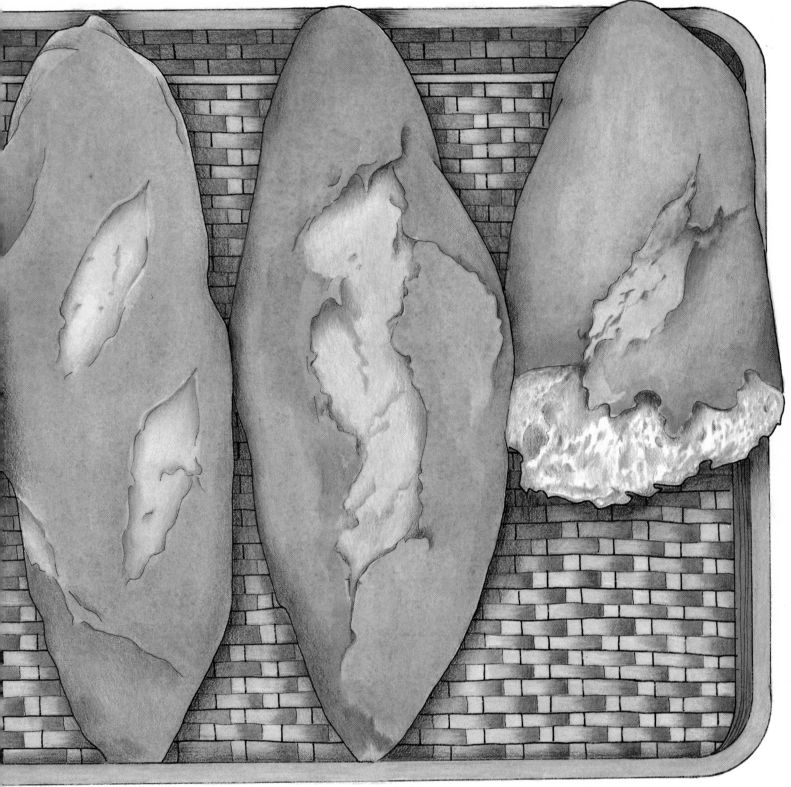

a SCHOOL of fish

a GAM of whales

a **FLEET** of ships
with
purple sails

a
CLUSTER
of
grapes

a
BEVY
of
beauties

.

all different
shapes

a **MUSTER** of peacocks

a
FLOCK
of
sheep

a
HOST
of
angels
fast
asleep

a BOUQUET
of flowers

a
SWARM
of
bees

a **KINDLE** of kittens
a
POD
of peas

a **PARCEL** of
penguins

a
FOREST
of
trees

a
COVEN
of
witches
as
scary
as
these

a **CLUMP**
of reeds

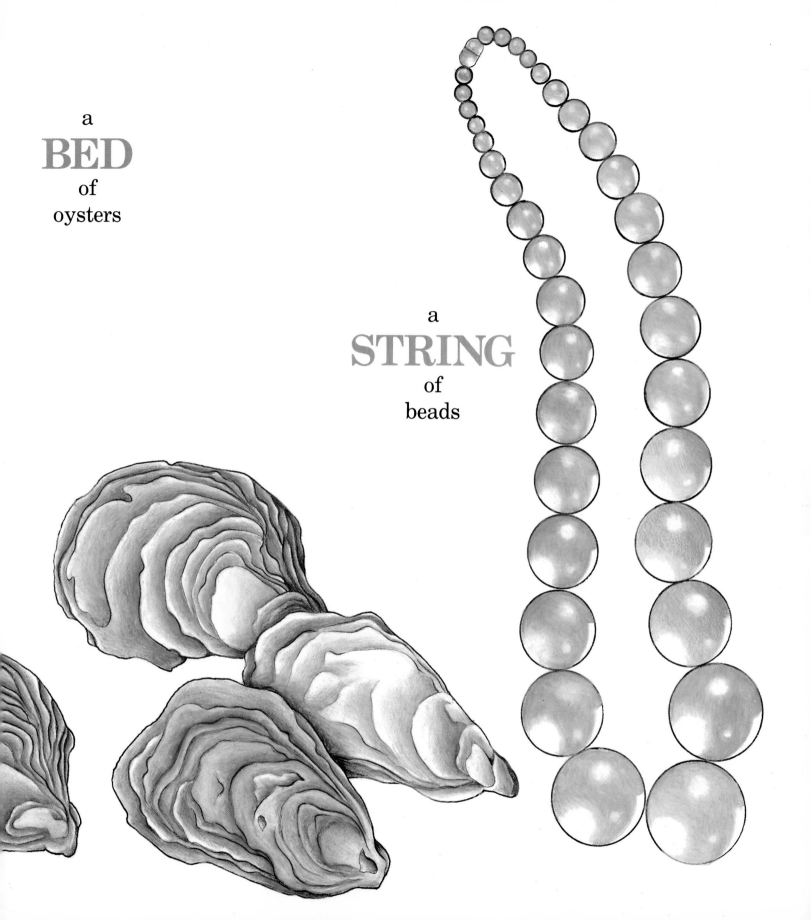

a
BED
of
oysters

a
STRING
of
beads

a
BROOD
of
chicks

a
CLUTCH
of
eggs

a
LITTER
of puppies on wobbly legs

a
PRIDE
of lions

a **LOCK** of hair

an
ARMY
of ants
from
here to…

there....

About five hundred years ago
knights and ladies in the know
used only very special words
to describe their flocks or herds.

These words are used by us today,
but some were lost along the way,
and new ones have been added too.

I've included quite a few.

And there are more of these group terms
like sleuth of bears
or clew of worms
or rafter of turkeys
walk of snails
leap of leopards
covey of quails.

But nouns aren't all collective,
and if I'm to be effective,
I'll tell about the other nouns
and adjectives and verbs.

All of them are parts of speech.

What fun!
I'll write a book for each.

—*Ruth Heller*

<u>Note:</u> One collective noun can describe many groups, as in a **host** of angels, daffodils, monks, thoughts, or sparrows.

One group can be described by more than one collective noun as in a **gam** of whales, a **mob** of whales, a **pod** of whales, a **school** of whales, or a **run** of whales.

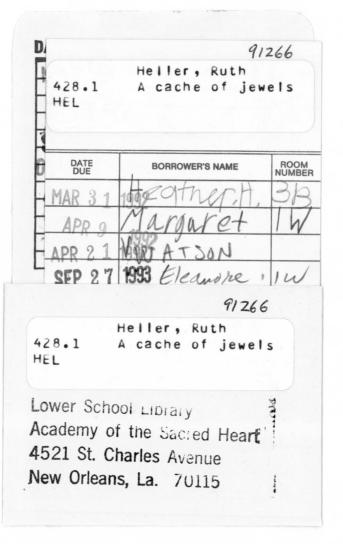

91266

Heller, Ruth
428.1   A cache of jewels
HEL

DATE DUE	BORROWER'S NAME	ROOM NUMBER
MAR 3 1 1992	Heather.H.	3B
APR 9	Margaret	1W
APR 2 1 1992	WATSON	
SEP 27 1993	Eleanore	1W

91266

Heller, Ruth
428.1   A cache of jewels
HEL